CONTENTS

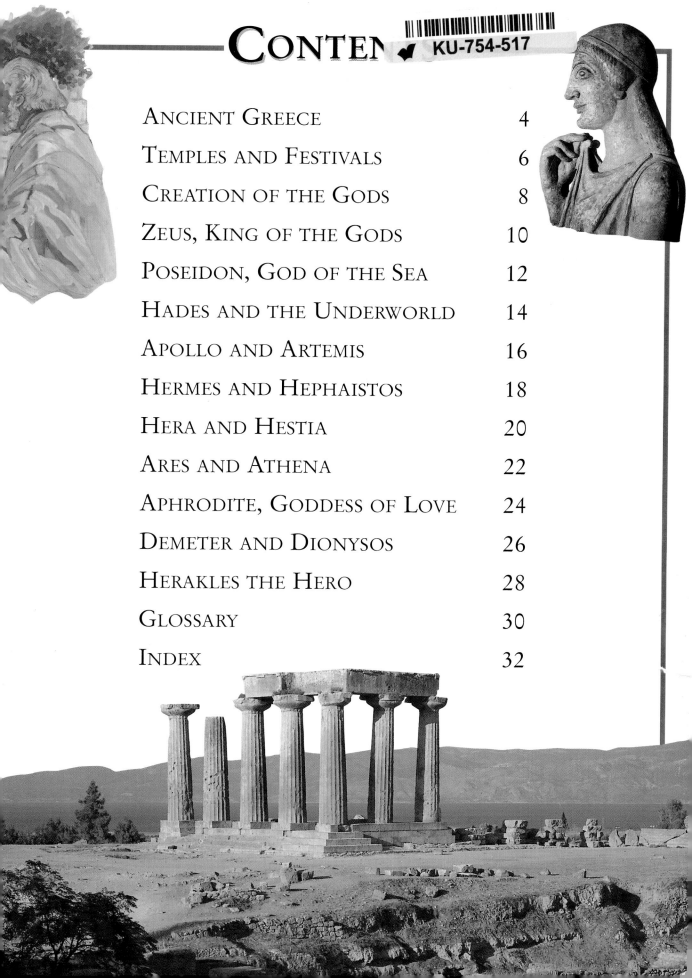

ANCIENT GREECE

GREECE IS a country by the Aegean Sea. It consists of a mainland and many islands. In ancient times it was not a single country as it is today. It was a collection of city-states. Each city and its surrounding countryside was an independent state. Each was ruled by a small group of powerful men, with a council elected by the citizens to make laws. The two most powerful cities were Athens and Sparta.

Greece had a sunny climate and plenty of food. People lived by farming, fishing and trading with their neighbours. They also fought with their neighbours. But all the Greeks spoke the same language. They told the same stories and worshipped the same gods. Foreigners were called 'barbarians' (uncivilized) because they did not speak Greek.

The Greeks believed that gods and goddesses watched over them, controlling events on earth. The gods commanded nature, the weather, the sea and the growth of farm crops. They could bring success or disaster to people. The gods were immortal – they lived forever – but like ordinary men and women they fell in love, felt jealous, and often behaved badly.

MYTHS, MONSTERS AND HEROES

Greek myths tell tales of hundreds of different gods. Many were linked to the heavens, like Helios, seen on this ancient coin, who was a sun god. Many were linked to nature. Woods, mountains and streams were the homes of nature spirits, who might be part human, part animal and part magical. There were stories of horrible monsters, and of superhuman heroes who had adventures in faraway places. Some tales explained how the world came to be as it is. Others were a mix of real events, religious teachings and adventure stories.

▼ The sea played an important part in the lives of the Greeks, but they rarely sailed out of sight of the land.

◀ The ancient Greeks carved lifelike statues. This young girl is making an offering to a goddess.

FAMILY OF THE GREEK GODS

KRONOS
youngest of the 12 Titans

APHRODITE
*goddess of love
and wife of
Hephaistos*

HESTIA
*goddess of
the hearth*

DEMETER
*goddess of
crops*

ZEUS
*king of the
gods and god
of the sky*

=

HERA
*goddess of
marriage*

POSEIDON
*god of the
sea*

HADES
*god of the
underworld*

ATHENA
*goddess of
wisdom and
war*

HERMES
*messenger of
the gods*

PERSEPHONE
*queen of the
underworld
and goddess of
plenty*

HEPHAISTOS
*smith god
and husband
of Aphrodite*

DIONYSOS
*god of wine
and revelry*

APOLLO
*god of
music,
poetry and
purity*

ARTEMIS
*goddess
of hunting*

HERAKLES
*demigod
and hero*

HEBE
*goddess of
youth*

ARES
*god of war
and lover
of
Aphrodite*

= MARRIAGE

▲ A family tree of some of the Greek gods. The most important were the twelve Olympians: Aphrodite, Apollo, Ares, Artemis, Athena, Demeter, Hephaistos, Hera, Hermes, Hestia, Poseidon, and Zeus, king of the gods. Zeus's brother Hades was ruler of the underworld. If you are unsure how to pronounce any of the names, look on page 31.

TEMPLES AND FESTIVALS

THE GREEKS carved fine statues of their gods and goddesses, and built magnificent temples for them. Priests looked after the temple and the god. People went to the temples to pray for help, taking gifts of money, flowers, food or wine. Each city had its patron – a defender god or goddess whose temple was often on a hilltop.

FESTIVALS AND GAMES

The Greeks held many religious festivals, which were like sports days, concerts and parties rolled into one. Crowds gathered to sing, recite poems, watch plays, dance and compete in athletic games. The first Olympic Games, held in 776BC, honoured Zeus, king of the gods. Three other great festivals were the Isthmian, Nemean and Pythian games. Many cities staged their own festivals every two to four years, honouring local gods and goddesses.

▼ Part of the Parthenon, the most famous Greek temple, which has suffered much damage since it was built between 447 and 432BC.

PROCESSIONS

The people of Athens built a temple to their patron goddess, Athena (see page 22), on a hill called the Acropolis. It was called the Parthenon. Men, women and

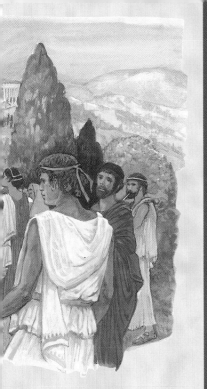

▲ The most famous oracle was at Delphi, in the mountains of central Greece. The priestess there – known as the Pythia – spoke for the god Apollo, giving her answers in verse.

children climbed the paths to the temple for festivals, leading sheep, goats or bulls for sacrifice, and carrying baskets of fruit and flowers with jars of wine and olive oil.

ORACLES

A person wanting to know the future ('will my baby be a boy?'), or the truth ('who stole my wine jars?') went to special shrines called oracles. Visitors asked the oracle questions, and in return for payment, the priest or priestess gave answers. Often the answers were riddles or could have more than one meaning.

▼ Greek athletes trained their bodies to be strong and beautiful. Competitors in all events were naked. Women were not allowed to watch.

GODS ON THE MOUNTAIN

The highest point in Greece is Mount Olympus. Above this cloud-topped mountain was the home of the gods. Heavenly Olympus was entered through a gate of clouds.

Inside, the gods all had their own palaces in which they spent endless days of pleasure while gazing down on ordinary mortals below. They feasted on nectar and a magical food called ambrosia, and remained forever handsome.

CREATION OF THE GODS

IN THE beginning, wrote the Greek poet Hesiod, there was Chaos – open, empty space. Out of this emptiness came Gaia, the earth. Later came Night and Day, and Eros (Love). To explain how the world of the gods came into being, Greek stories told of struggles between old and new gods.

FIRST FAMILY
Gaia produced the first

▶ Oceanos, shown in this Roman mosaic, was leader of the Titans, the oldest family of Greek gods.

BIRTH OF APHRODITE
Kronos attacked his father Uranos as he slept. His blood dripped onto the earth where the Furies – three goddesses of vengeance – sprang from its drops. As the wounded Titan bled onto the waves of the sea, white foam sparkled, and from this foam was born the most beautiful of all goddesses, Aphrodite (see page 24), seen here as Roman Venus in this famous painting by the Italian artist Botticelli.

▲ A marble head of a Cyclops, with its single eye on the bridge of its nose.

family of gods. She gave birth to Uranos, the sky and stars, and also to Pontos, the sea. Gaia and her son Uranos then bred the first race of superbeings – the twelve Titans.

Uranos and Gaia had three more children, the one-eyed Cyclopes, and three terrible monsters called the Hekatonchires, each of which had 100 arms and 50 heads.

FAMILY BREAK-UP

Uranos was so horrified by his child-monsters that he hid them in the dark centre of the earth. This made Gaia angry, and she plotted revenge. She persuaded her youngest son Kronos to attack his father with a sharp knife. Uranos was left wounded and powerless, and Kronos became ruler of the sky. He married his sister Rhea, and they had six children. The girls were Hestia, Demeter and Hera; the sons were Hades, Poseidon and Zeus.

Despite her cruelty, Gaia was loved by the Greeks. She was mother of the human race, and goddess of marriage and fertility – the earth mother.

BIRTH OF ZEUS

Zeus was the sixth child of Kronos. The five children before him had been swallowed by their father as soon as they were born. Zeus's mother, Rhea, asked Uranos and Gaia for help to save her sixth child. They hid Rhea in a cave, where she gave birth to the baby Zeus. To trick Kronos, Rhea wrapped a stone in baby clothes and gave it to her husband to swallow. This 17th-century German woodcut shows Kronos in the heavens consuming his child, while ordinary mortals go about their business down below.

Z EUS WAS king of the gods, the giver of justice. His right hand held a thunderbolt, which he threw to punish those who broke his laws. An eagle was his messenger and, being a sky god, mountains and tall trees were held sacred to him.

ZEUS OVERTHROWS HIS FATHER

Zeus grew up in the forests, hidden from his father, Kronos. He was cared for by a goat named Amaltheia. In the goat's honour, Zeus made a magical goatskin cloak to protect him; it became his sacred aegis, the sign of his godliness.

Grown to manhood, Zeus tricked Kronos into drinking a potion that made the old god sick, so that he vomited up his five elder children, still alive. Kronos was then banished, and Zeus took his place.

OLYMPIANS AT WAR

With his five brothers and sisters, Zeus set up his kingdom on Mount Olympus. But the old Titans attacked the new gods and war raged for ten years. Zeus freed the Hekatonchires and the Cyclopes and these monsters helped defeat the Titans who were banished to the depths of the earth.

ZEUS'S KINGDOM

Zeus shared his power

GIFTS FOR THE GODS

Zeus was protector of the home, of guests and strangers. Pilgrims climbed to his mountain-top shrines, built as near to Zeus as was possible on earth. Families put statues of Zeus and other gods in front of their houses, with altars on which they left offerings of food, wine and flowers.

PROMETHEUS ANGERS ZEUS

Prometheus was a Titan who did not join the war against the Olympians. But he made Zeus angry by stealing fire from the gods and giving it to humans. As a punishment, Prometheus was chained to a rock. An eagle flew down each day to tear out his liver, which grew afresh each night. His torment lasted hundreds of years, until Herakles (see page 28) killed the eagle and freed him.

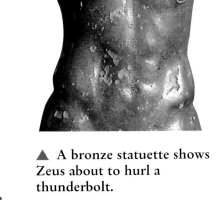

▲ A bronze statuette shows Zeus about to hurl a thunderbolt.

▶ After the battle with the Titans, Zeus was attacked by the giant, serpent-legged monsters sprung from the blood of Uranos. This is how a 20th-century artist shows the battle.

with his brothers and sisters. Poseidon was given the sea as his realm and Hades was to rule the underworld. Zeus first married Metis, but his second wife and queen was Hera (see page 20). However, he also had numerous children with other women. To pursue his many love affairs, Zeus often changed shape, doing his wooing as a human or even as an animal.

Zeus never hesitated to use his godly powers when a woman caught his eye. To win Leda, the mother of Helen of Troy (see page 24), he turned himself into a swan.

▲ A magnificent statue of Zeus in the temple at Olympia was made about 435BC by the sculptor Pheidias. It was one of the Seven Wonders of the Ancient World. This 19th-century woodcut shows what it must have looked like.

POSEIDON, GOD OF THE SEA

POSEIDON WAS Zeus's brother. He was as wild and unruly as the ocean waves he ruled, and people believed he also caused earthquakes on land. He lived beneath the Aegean Sea, in a magnificent underwater palace. He rode over the waves in a chariot pulled by horses, surrounded by Tritons and playful sea monsters.

Poseidon was the god of horses, of sea creatures, and freshwater springs. Pictures of him show a stern figure with an untidy beard, bare-chested and grasping a three-pronged fishing spear or trident.

POSEIDON AND MEDUSA

Poseidon had changed himself into a horse. In this form, he fell in love with the winged monster Medusa. As a result of their union, Medusa gave birth to the flying horse Pegasus. But Medusa and Poseidon had used the temple of Athena for their lovemaking, and Athena was enraged by this insult to her holy temple. To punish Medusa she turned her hair into snakes!

TROUBLEMAKER AND LOVER

Poseidon was always seeking to make more of his kingdom, by stealing lands from other gods and goddesses. Forced to obey Zeus, he constantly grumbled. When he tried to revolt, Zeus made him build the city walls of Troy as a punishment.

SEA PEOPLE AND PIRATES

The Greeks were a sea people. Many of them made their living as fishermen or traders, sailing from mainland ports and between the many islands of the Aegean Sea. They feared and respected the power

▼ Poseidon's temple at Cape Sounion overlooked the sea.

Like Zeus, Poseidon was unfaithful to his wife, Amphitrite, and chased after the goddesses of Olympus. Demeter had to change herself into a horse to escape him, but crafty Poseidon caught up with her by becoming a stallion.

f the sea and its mighty uler. They also feared irates, whose fast warships ould overtake them. To vin Poseidon's favour, eople made offerings of ulls. In one ceremony as nany as 80 bulls might e sacrificed, and hen eaten.

▲ Poseidon had many savage children. Among them was Polyphemus, the Cyclops, whom Odysseus met and defeated on his travels.

▼ This bronze statue shows one or other of the brother gods, Poseidon or Zeus.

SEA GODS

Pontos ancient sea god from the beginning of time.
Oceanos father of all rivers.
Nereus a kindly Old Man of the Sea, who lived with his wife Doris beneath the Aegean Sea.
Nereids fifty beautiful sea nymphs, the daughters of Nereus.
Proteus sea god who guarded Poseidon's seals.
Glaucos fisherman who became a god and would appear to sailors, usually to give bad news.
Tritons half-men and half-fish, blowing conch shell trumpets; the original Triton was the son of Poseidon and Amphitrite.
Sirens lured sailors onto the rocks with their beautiful singing (below).

HADES AND THE UNDERWORLD

THE GREEKS thought the grave was a gateway to a gloomy underworld ruled by Zeus's brother, Hades. This shadowy king seldom visited the upper world, but when he did, he became invisible.

HADES' KINGDOM

Hades ruled a sad kingdom, in which the dead wandered without hope. Once a soul had drunk from the underworld river Lethe, all memory of the past was forgotten. In the underworld, people became 'shades', ghostly shadows of their former selves.

Some Greeks hoped their souls might find a happier afterlife, in a kind of paradise called the Elysian Fields. They also believed there was a kind of Hell for wicked people. The worst of these, or those who displeased the gods, were sent for ever to the fiery depths of Tartarus deep beneath the earth.

▲ Orpheus descended into the underworld and played his lyre to persuade Hades to let him take his dead wife, Eurydice, back to earth.

CAKES FOR CERBERUS

A funeral procession marked the passing of a person's soul from the sunlit upper world into the shadows of Hades' kingdom. Family and friends would praise the dead person, and his or her ancestors. The guests made offerings of bowls of warm milk and small bottles of consecrated (blessed) blood. They put food and drink for the dead person into the grave, and some honey cakes as tasty morsels for Cerberus.

◄ This statue shows Hades with his wife Persephone and Cerberus, his three-headed dog.

CERBERUS AND CHARON

Whether a person died peacefully in old age or heroically in battle, the same fate awaited them – the underworld.

At the gates of the underworld stood the three-headed watchdog Cerberus, who allowed all to enter but none to leave. The dead person then had to cross three underground rivers: Acheron, Lethe, and finally Styx. A bad-tempered ferryman named Charon demanded money to take his boat. So when anybody died, a coin was placed in their mouth to pay the ferryman.

▶ This carving shows Charon the boatman demanding his fares for ferrying two dead souls across the river Styx.

APOLLO AND ARTEMIS

THE SUN was giver of life and energy. Apollo the sun-god was the most splendid of all. His twin sister Artemis was goddess of the moon.

APOLLO, THE FAVOURED GOD

Every Greek loved and feared Apollo. He was the son of Zeus and Leto, a Titan goddess, and was almost as powerful as his father. He was strong and handsome, wise and just. He let people know when they had done wrong, and

APOLLO AND DAPHNE

Apollo once made fun of Eros (see page 24), who was proud of his skill with bow and arrow. Eros got his own back by shooting the god with a gold-tipped arrow that made him fall in love with a river nymph named Daphne. He shot Daphne with a lead-tipped arrow, which made her flee in terror at the sight of Apollo. Apollo chased her and would not give up, until Gaia took pity on Daphne and turned her into a laurel tree!

▶ A huntsman named Actaeon spied on Artemis as she was bathing. Artemis was so angry, she turned him into a stag. The animal fled, but was torn to pieces by her hounds. This vase painting shows a hunter and his dog.

▼ This Roman carving shows the nine muses. These daughters of Zeus and Mnemosyne, goddess of memory, each looked after one of the arts or sciences.

SPREADING CIVILIZATION

The Greeks spread their ideas and way of life all around the Mediterranean where they set up colonies. They built

could cleanse their sins if they were truly sorry. The god spoke to people at his oracle (see page 7).

Apollo had many qualities. He was leader of the nine muses, goddesses who looked after the arts and sciences, and who could also see the future. He played the lyre, a stringed instrument on which he produced music of unearthly beauty. He was god of medicine, music, poetry and dance.

HUNTING GODDESS

Apollo's sister Artemis helped at her twin brother's birth – and was ever after the goddess of childbirth. She was also the spirit of nature, of plants and trees, and of the wild animals she hunted with bow and arrow.

Artemis was so beautiful that every god wanted to marry her, but the goddess refused them all. She liked to roam free. Every evening she drove a chariot led by white horses across the starry sky.

LIGHT OF THE MOON

Artemis fell in love with a shepherd called Endymion and kissed him while he slept. This was unlucky for the poor man. Waking as if from a dream, Endymion was offered this choice by Zeus: death or eternal sleep in a cave beneath a mountain. The shepherd chose sleep. In his slumber, he was visited every night by Artemis who watched over his flocks by moonlight.

...emples and theatres and ...rought with them poetry ...nd plays, music, dancing, ...nd all the arts dear to ...pollo. People flocked to ...ee comic and tragic plays ...n huge outdoor theatres.

HERMES AND HEPHAISTOS

WHEN PEOPLE needed help with ordinary workaday matters, they called upon slow, stolid Hephaistos and his fleet-footed brother Hermes. While Hephaistos was the smith of the gods and god of fire, his brother was god of travellers, traders – and thieves.

SMITH TO THE GODS

Most gods were handsome, but not Hephaistos. He was lame, and so ugly as a child that his mother Hera threw him out of Olympus. He fell into the sea, and was rescued by the Nereids, the daughters of Nereus, a sea god.

In exile, Hephaistos learned his craft well, becoming the most skilled metalsmith. He made arrows for Apollo and Artemis, a sword for the hero Perseus, and armour for the warrior Achilles.

The other gods made fun of Hephaistos, but ordinary people and workers in many trades looked on him as their friend. People swore they could hear his laugh when

▲ A vase painting of smi[th] in a forge, where they ma[de] tools, weapons and armou[r]

MAGIC CHAIR

Hephaistos made a magic chair of gold to give to his unkind mother Hera. As soon as she sat down, the chair held her fast. No god could free her. She stayed stuck in the chair until Dionysos, god of wine, made Hephaistos drunk and got him to set his mother free.

◄ The Greeks loved hardworking Hephaistos. In this vase painting of him on his horse, you can see his lame feet.

► Hermes wore winged sandals and a winged hat. These helped him travel the world in the twinkling of an eye, carrying messages for the gods.

MASTER CRAFTSMEN

The Greeks were fine artists and masters of many crafts and skills. Architects created elegant temples, sculptors carved lifelike statues and friezes of gods and humans, potters made clay vases that painters decorated with scenes from mythology. In their workshops, craftsmen and slaves produced metal goods, armour, clothes and jewellery. Women spun thread and wove cloth in the home. In dockyards, shipbuilders constructed sturdy wooden ships to carry all these goods for trade.

▲ When he was still a baby, clever Hermes made the first lyre, from a tortoise shell. He gave it to Apollo, seen here in this wall painting, to make up for a quarrel.

firewood crackled on the hearth. They believed that smiths, like him, had magical skills. In the heat and fire of the forge, they turned dull metal into farming tools and gleaming weapons and armour for warriors.

MESSENGER OF THE GODS

Hermes was the youngest son of Zeus and a goddess named Maia. He was fond of practical jokes, but always willing to help gods and mortals with his quick wits and cheek. To bring good luck, people in Athens set up a stone head of Hermes on a pillar outside the front door. Statues of him were placed at crossroads, to guide wayfarers along the right road. Hermes even escorted the souls of the dead to Hades. Since most travel was for trade, Hermes became the god of traders. But the Greeks were wary of fast-talking salesmen, and made Hermes god of thieves and gamblers, as well.

HERMES AND APOLLO'S OXEN

As a child, Hermes stole some oxen from his big brother Apollo. To hide the theft, the rascal drove the animals backwards, so their hoofprints appeared to go in the opposite direction. Nevertheless Apollo caught him and complained to their father. Hermes claimed not even to know what an ox was. Zeus was amused at his cheek and let him off, provided he became messenger of the gods and made peace with Apollo.

HERA AND HESTIA

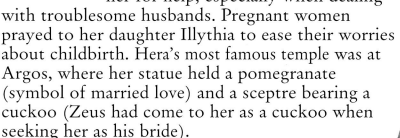

HERA, WIFE of Zeus, was queen of the gods. Women looked to her for help, especially when dealing with troublesome husbands. Pregnant women prayed to her daughter Illythia to ease their worries about childbirth. Hera's most famous temple was at Argos, where her statue held a pomegranate (symbol of married love) and a sceptre bearing a cuckoo (Zeus had come to her as a cuckoo when seeking her as his bride).

QUEEN OF THE OLYMPIANS

The married life of Hera and Zeus was stormy. He was always falling in love with other women, and in his rages he hurled thunderbolts at his wife. She in her turn nagged and plotted. Despite such troubles, Hera was honoured as Zeus's queen. She controlled the weather and so was important to farmers. Women asked Hera to help with everyday problems – and to grant them a married life happier than her own.

GODDESS AND HER MONSTER CHILD

When Zeus produced a daughter, Athena, from his own head, Hera was furious. She sought aid from the banished Titans to produce a similar child herself. The result was a terrible multi-headed monster, Typhon. Zeus punished her by hanging Hera from the sky in chains.

Hestia bustled about the ome, looking after the amily, answering people's rayers for peace and plenty round their hearth.

This picture, painted on plate, shows Hera earing a cloak, and the iadem and sceptre of a ueen. She is often shown ith a peacock, called rgos.

FOUNTAIN OF HEALTH

Sick people believed that illness was a divine punishment. Some took part in purification ceremonies before sacrificing a bull at a temple. They then spent the night sleeping on the bull's skin and hoping that Asklepios would come in a dream with a cure. The temple priest explained what the dream meant. People paid for his advice by tossing coins into the temple fountain. The priest was also a doctor, so 'miraculous' cures were not unusual.

HESTIA OF THE HEARTH

Family life, warmth and security centred on the home – and at its heart lay the fire burning on the hearth. Its goddess was Hestia, who was more gentle than Hera. Having refused both Poseidon and Apollo, she had no husband to vex her. As goddess of domestic life, she was also seen as a protector of the whole community.

▶ Unless they had slaves, women did most of the work in the home.

HEALING THE SICK

Several gods had healing powers. One was Apollo, another was his son Asklepios, an elderly god who was helped by his daughter Hygeia. Asklepios learned his healing skill from the wise centaur, Chiron. Temples to him were built outside towns on what people thought were the healthiest spots. The priests of these temples gave out advice and medicines, and passed on medical knowledge from father to son. In this carving, Asklepios and Hygeia receive offerings at their altar.

ARES AND ATHENA

THE GREEKS were often at war. Rival city-states fought one another, or joined forces against foreign enemies such as the Trojans and the Persians. People admired great heroes, like Achilles and Ajax, but not Ares, the god of war: he was too bloodthirsty and untrustworthy. The goddess Athena, skilled in the arts of war, was loved by all. People called on them both when danger threatened.

THE GOD NOBODY LOVED

Ares was the complete opposite of his half-brother Apollo. Nobody loved him, not even his father Zeus nor his mother Hera (whom Zeus blamed for Ares' bad temper). He was boastful, enjoyed slaughter not justice, and was always ready to change sides in battle. He looked fierce – a giant with a roar louder than the shouts of 10,000 men. But he was a bad loser. When the goddess Athena knocked him down with a stone, he ran to his father Zeus, whining that she did not fight fair.

ATHENA THE WISE WARRIOR

Athena, goddess of wisdom, was honoured throughout Greece, but especially in Athens, the city she protected. Though she was terrible in her anger, she defended good against evil and was always victorious in battle. She brought death to many, but people saw

◀ This painting of Ares is by the 16th-century Italian painter Veronese.

▼ Arachne boasted that she could outshine Athena at weaving. Of course Arachne lost the competition and Athena turned her into a spider.

GODS ON THE WINNING SIDE

All Greek citizens had to fight for their state. Boys were taught combat skills so that they could serve in the army or navy, or as oarsmen on warships. They had to provide their own weapons and armour. Foot soldiers called hoplites wore breastplates, leg armour, helmets and shields. They carried swords and spears. There were also archers, javelin throwers, charioteers and some cavalry. Rival armies prayed to the same gods, and complained when the gods seemed to favour the enemy.

Statues of Athena, known as palladia, were said to have fallen from heaven. Owning one gave you special protection.

It was Athena's idea to trick the Trojans by giving them a wooden horse in which were hidden Greek soldiers.

her as a creator and not a destroyer. Her tree was the olive, its branch a symbol of peace.

GODDESS OF CRAFTS

Athena, like Apollo, had many talents. She was the goddess of crafts, the inventor of ploughing, spinning, weaving and pottery. She tamed horses and, during the Trojan War, showed the Greeks how to make the Wooden Horse. Hidden inside the horse, Greek soldiers tricked their way into the city of Troy. She also helped build the ship in which Jason went exploring with the Argonauts. Above all, she excelled at women's skills, such as sewing and weaving.

STRANGE BIRTH

Athena was the daughter of Zeus and his first wife, Metis. Convinced that she would have a son who would challenge his rule, Zeus swallowed the unborn child. When the baby was ready to be born, Zeus suffered terrible head pains. He staggered about, roaring in agony. Hermes told Hephaistos to split open Zeus's head with an axe, and out sprang the goddess Athena – full-grown and wearing armour. Athena became her father's favourite. She never married, which is why the people of Athens called her 'Parthenos', meaning 'Virgin'.

APHRODITE, GODDESS OF LOVE

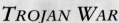

WHEN A woman wanted a husband or a baby, she prayed to Aphrodite, the goddess of love. She was first and foremost a fertility goddess and no one doubted her powers. She was more beautiful than any of her countless statues. As well as blessing marriages (and calming storms), she could make both gods and mortals mad with passions that destroyed them.

Aphrodite was born from the foaming blood of the old god Uranos, and rose naked from the waves (see page 8). She floated on a shell until she came to the island of Cyprus, where she made her earthly home.

LOVE MUDDLES ALL

Love was Aphrodite's only interest. In her schemes, she was aided by Eros, who in some stories is said to be her son. Zeus gave Aphrodite as wife to Hephaistos (see page 18), but she did not love him. She preferred the brutal Ares, god of war. Hephaistos spied on them, flung a net over the lovers, and dragged them before the other gods, who laughed heartily at their embarrassment.

▲ Eros sharpens his golden arrow in this 18th-century painting, which shows the god as a chubby baby.

TROJAN WAR
Helen of Troy was a daughter of Zeus, who had wooed her mother Leda in the form of a swan. Amazingly beautiful, Helen was already married to Menelaus, king of Sparta, when Paris carried her off to Troy. Menelaus gave chase, and so began the ten-year Trojan War. Here Menelaus regains his wife after the capture of Troy.

PARIS JUDGES A BEAUTY CONTEST

Hera and Athena were rivals to Aphrodite in beauty. Rather than make the choice himself, Zeus asked Paris, Prince of Troy, to choose the loveliest of the three goddesses. Hera tried to bribe Paris, by offering him all of Asia. Athena promised that he would win every battle. Aphrodite simply stepped out of her tunic and promised Paris the most beautiful of all mortal women as his bride. Paris awarded Aphrodite the prize of a golden apple and so won the lovely Helen of Troy (see panel opposite).

PYGMALION AND GALATEA

Aphrodite was often cruel, but she could be kind. A sculptor named Pygmalion made an ivory statue of her, so lifelike that he fell in love with it. He asked Aphrodite to give him a wife as beautiful as the carved figure. Rather than do this, the goddess made the statue come to life, as Galatea, a human copy of herself. Pygmalion married Galatea, seen in this painting riding the waves like Aphrodite.

WOMEN AND CHILDREN

Most girls married in their mid-teens, but their husbands were usually older and chosen for them. Throughout her life a woman was in the keeping of a male relative – father, brother, husband, son. Women ran the household and did most of the work in the home. Greek parents did not want to have too many children. Even well-off couples complained of the expense. They had to keep slaves to look after them, provide them with education and, in the case of girls, a dowry (gift) when they married.

◀ This statue of Aphrodite shows her squeezing the water from her hair after she has risen from her bath.

DEMETER AND DIONYSOS

DEMETER, sister of Zeus, was goddess of the soil and of the harvest. This kind and generous goddess did not have a happy life. Her daughter Persephone (or Kore) had the misfortune to catch the eye of Hades, who carried her off to the underworld. Demeter begged Hades to let her daughter go, but he refused. In the end, a bargain was struck that let Persephone live in the sunlight for half of the year. When she returned to the underworld, Demeter grieved and the fields were bare. Only when Persephone came back to her mother did new green shoots burst through the earth again.

DRUNKEN REVELLERS
Dionysos was a son of Zeus and Semele, a mortal who shrivelled to ashes when she dared to look on Zeus in his full glory.

MIDAS AND THE GOLDEN TOUCH
King Midas of Phrygia once helped the old satyr Silenus. Dionysos offered him a reward, and Midas asked 'Let everything I touch turn to gold'. And so they did – stones, flowers, clothes, food and drink – even his own daughter. Panic-stricken, Midas begged to be spared before he starved to death. Dionysos told him to leap into a river, and the water washed away the curse of the golden touch. This illustration by Walter Crane shows Midas with his daughter.

COUNTRY LIFE
Most Greeks were farmers, though there was little good soil, and hot, dry summers parched the land. Townspeople like Homer wrote of carefree merrymaking and peaceful fields with grazing flocks,

◀ People thanked Demeter with gifts at harvest festivals, and the first loaf made from new flour was dedicated to her.

▶ A vase painting shows Dionysos with his drinking horn. Worship of Dionysos became a cult and his drunken followers often caused trouble.

uit-laden orchards and shady live groves. The farmer-poet Hesiod was more honest about country life, describing his village as miserable, with weather that was bad in winter and worse in summer.

Dionysos was only a demigod and did not live on Olympus. To escape jealous Hera, he was brought up by mountain nymphs. His tutor was Silenus, an old satyr (half-man, half-goat), who taught him how to make wine. Dionysos then became god of wine.

Vengeful Hera put a curse on Dionysos, dooming him to roam, dancing and singing, without rest. He shared his wine with a band of noisy revellers – Silenus, nymphs, humans (especially women called maenads), centaurs and other half-humans. This drunken rabble romped through many lands, planting grapes as they went.

PAN, GOD OF NATURE

The goatish god Pan had no place among the elegant gods of Mount Olympus. He was far older, and so ugly that even his mother fled from the sight of him. He chased any maiden who caught his eye and could send people half-mad with fear. From his name comes our word 'panic'. Fortunately, Pan liked to laze in the afternoon heat. He might be glimpsed dozing under a tree or playing a tune on his pipes to soothe the sheep and cattle grazing nearby.

HERAKLES THE HERO

THE CALM of everyday life was disturbed from time to time by wars or disasters. Tales were told of terrifying monsters and tyrants. Then there was need for a hero: a warrior brave and clever enough to slay monsters, rescue maidens, and even outwit the gods themselves. Many of these heroes were sons of Zeus.

HERAKLES THE DEMIGOD

The most famous hero was Herakles (the Romans called him Hercules). He was the son of Zeus and Alcmene, queen of Thebes. As a baby, he showed his strength by strangling two snakes sent by Hera to attack him and his twin brother Iphicles. He grew up to be a man of godlike strength and appetite, who could devour a whole ox in one meal. He married Hebe, the goddess of eternal youth.

ANGRY QUEEN

Hera was Herakles' eternal foe. She drove him mad, so that he killed his first wife, his children, and his brother's children. For this crime, he was banished, and made to serve a mean and unpleasant king named Eurystheus. He made Herakles carry

◀ In this 18th-century painting, the baby Herakles strangles snakes sent by Hera to kill him.

▶ This is a marble statue of Herakles by the 1st-century BC Greek sculptor Glycon.

IDEAS MADE TO LAST

To honour their gods, the Greeks built the most beautiful buildings and sculptures. They told stories of them in poems and plays. The Greeks produced great thinkers: scientists, doctors

out twelve 'labours' (see panel). After the fourth, the cowardly king was so frightened by what Herakles could do that he hid inside a large jar whenever the hero returned!

His labours over, Herakles was free for further adventures. In the end he fell victim to a trick, set up by the centaur Nessos, and was poisoned. Writhing in agony, he begged to be burned to death. A shepherd lit his funeral fire, whereupon Zeus sent a lightning bolt from the heavens and claimed Herakles as a god, to live on Olympus.

...athematicians, historians ...d philosophers, and they ...vented democracy, still the ...eest form of government. ...reek ideas have had a lasting ...fluence, and people still ...njoy hearing the stories of ...eir gods.

ANOTHER HERO
Perseus was the brave son of Zeus and a maiden named Danae. He vowed to slay the Gorgon Medusa, whose gaze turned people to stone. Luckily for Perseus, Athena had given him a brightly polished shield. He used this as a mirror to look at Medusa's reflection – not directly at her terrifying face – while he struck off her head with his sword. Flying home, with the aid of magical winged sandals, Perseus saved a princess named Andromeda from a sea serpent.

LABOURS OF HERAKLES

1. Killing the lion of Nemea with his bare hands. Herakles wore its skin always, to protect him.
2. Killing the Hydra, a monster with nine poison-breathing heads. He tipped his arrows with its venom.
3. Catching alive the hind (female deer) of Ceryneia after a year-long chase.
4. Catching the Erymanthian boar, again alive.
5. Cleaning out the overflowing stables and cowsheds of Augeias, King of Elis. Herakles did this in a day, by diverting two rivers to wash away the muck.
6. Shooting a flock of man-eating birds at Stymphalus; first putting them to flight with clashing cymbals given him by Athena.
7. Fetching a huge bull from the island of Crete.
8. Taming the wild mares of King Diomedes, horses so savage they ate human flesh.
9. Stealing a golden girdle from Hippolyte, queen of the Amazons, a race of warrior women.
10. Fetching the cattle of the three-bodied monster Geryon from the western edge of the world.
11. Taking golden apples from a tree in the Garden of the Hesperides; after many adventures on the way, he had to slay the guardian dragon Ladon.
12. Carrying the three-headed dog Cerberus up from the underworld, and showing him to the terrified king (left).

GLOSSARY

aegis Shield or defensive armour, particularly of Zeus and Athena.

ambrosia Food of the gods.

BC Stands for 'before Christ', and is used for all year-dates before the birth of Jesus. AD stands for 'Anno Domini' (in the year of our Lord), which is used for all year-dates after the birth of Jesus.

centaur Legendary creature with a horse's body and a human head; the most famous centaur was Chiron.

chariot Kind of cart, usually two-wheeled, pulled by animals.

city-state Any important city with its own independent government which ruled the surrounding region. Examples are Athens, Thebes and Sparta.

cult Belief or form of religious worship, often kept secret from other people.

curse Evil spell, bringing bad luck or even death.

demigod Half-god, with one mortal and one god parent.

demon Evil spirit, like a devil, often found in the underworld, or hell.

divine Of the gods, godlike.

dowry Property or money given by a bride's family to the bridegroom.

ferryman Person who ferries people across a river in a boat for a fee.

fertile Able to grow crops or (in a human) able to have children.

festival Holiday in honour of a god, when people feast, dance, make music and parade through the streets to the temple.

forge Furnace, or workshop containing a furnace; or the act of heating and shaping metal.

frieze Band of stonework on a temple, sculpted with images of gods, or other decoration.

ghostly Like the spirit of the dead thought to return to the land of the living.

hearth Fireplace in the home.

hero Remarkable person, often of unusual courage and strength, who does exceptionally brave deeds.

hoplite Foot-soldier in Greek armies.

immortal Able to live for ever; gods were immortal, humans were not.

labour Task or job, usually involving much effort.

lyre Stringed instrument like a small harp.

mortal Human being, someone who is born and dies.

muses Nine goddesses of the arts and sciences.

myth Ancient story about gods and heroes, originally passed by word of mouth; some myths explain natural events, such as earthquakes.

nymph Fairylike being, a spirit of wild places (springs, rivers, woods).

oracle Person or thing through which people believed the gods communicated with humans.

oxen Large male cattle trained to pull ploughs or carts.

patron Someone who watches over others, or has the power to help them.

pilgrim Person who travels to a religious shrine or sacred place.

sacrifice Killing an animal or a person to thank a god or to obtain the god's favour.

satyrs Wild creatures, half human and half goat.

shrine Small temple or the most sacred area inside a larger temple.

smith Metalworker who forges tools and weapons in a forge.

soul Spirit believed in many religions to leave the body after death and travel to the next world.

temple Place of worship. In Greece, each god and goddess had his or her own temple.

thunderbolt Sign of a god's anger (particularly Zeus's), flung at people below, with the noise of thunder and the flash of lightning.

underworld The world of the dead, ruled by Hades.

virgin Person who has not had sex.

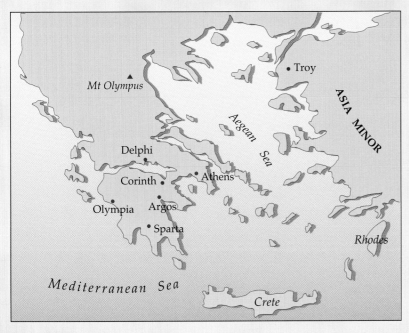

The map shows the mainland and islands of the country that is now Greece. In ancient times Greece comprised many separate city-states. Asia Minor is present-day Turkey.

HOW TO PRONOUNCE THE NAMES OF THE GREEK GODS

Aphrodite (Aff-ro-die-tee)

Apollo (A-poll-o; 'a' as in apple)

Ares (Air-eez)

Artemis (Are-tem-iss)

Athena (Ath-ee-na)

Demeter (Dem-ee-ta)

Dionysos (Die-on-eye-soss)

Gaia (Guy-ah)

Hades (Hay-deez)

Hebe (Hee-bee)

Hephaistos (Heff-aye-stoss)

Hera (Here-a)

Herakles (Hair-a-kleez)

Hermes (Her-meez)

Hestia (Hess-tee-a)

Kronos (Kron-oss)

Persephone (Per-seff-on-ee)

Poseidon (Poss-eye-don)

Uranos (Your-an-oss)

Zeus (Zz-youss; like juice)

MORE CHARACTERS FROM GREEK MYTHS

ARIADNE daughter of King Minos and lover of Theseus

CYCLOPES three one-eyed giants: Brontes (thunder), Steropes (lightning), Arges (thunderbolt)

DAEDALUS brilliant inventor who built the Labyrinth (maze), and wax wings to help his son Icarus fly

EOS goddess of dawn, sister of Helios

FATES or **FURIES** three terrible sisters: Klotho, who spun the thread of destiny, Lachesis, who measured out its length, Atropos, who cut the thread to end each person's life

FOUR WINDS Boreas (north), Zephyrus (west), Euros (east), Notos (south)

HEKATONCHIRES three fierce monsters: Kottos (furious), Briareos (vigorous), Gyges (big-limbed)

HELIOS god of the sun, son of Hyperion

ICARUS boy who tried to fly with wax wings, which melted in the sun's heat

MINOTAUR monster with bull's head that fed on live humans

MOROS invisible being who decreed what must be

MUSES nine goddesses who looked after arts and sciences: Calliope (epic poetry), Erato (love poetry), Euterpe (flute playing); Melpomene (tragedy), Thalia (comedy), Klio (history), Urania (astronomy), Polyhymnia (religious song and mime), Terpsichore (lyric poetry and dance)

PHAETON son of Helios, who drove his father's chariot across the sky

SELENE moon goddess, sister of Helios

THESEUS Athenian prince who killed the Minotaur in King Minos's Labyrinth

TITANS twelve 'old' gods: Uranos, Oceanos, Koeros, Hyperion, Krios, Iapetos, Theia, Rhea, Mnemosyne, Phoebe, Tethys, Themis

INDEX

Page numbers in *italics* refer to illustrations.